Francis Frith's
Around
Bridgwater

Photographic Memories

Francis Frith's
Around
Bridgwater

Toni Beet

First published in paperback in the United Kingdom in 2001 by
The Francis Frith Collection®

Paperback edition 2001 ISBN 1-85937-305-4
Reprinted in paperback 2006

Text and Design copyright The Francis Frith Collection®
Photographs copyright The Francis Frith Collection®
except where indicated.

The Frith® photographs and the Frith® logo are reproduced under licence from
Heritage Photographic Resources Ltd, the owners of the Frith® archive and trademarks.
'The Francis Frith Collection', 'Francis Frith' and 'Frith' are registered trademarks of
Heritage Photographic Resources Ltd.

All rights reserved. No photograph in this publication may be sold to a third party other
than in the original form of this publication, or framed for sale to a third party.
No parts of this publication may be reproduced, stored in a retrieval system, or transmitted,
in any form, or by any means, electronic, mechanical, photocopying, recording or otherwise,
without the prior permission of the publishers and copyright holder.

British Library Cataloguing in Publication Data

Around Bridgwater - Photographic Memories
Toni Beet
ISBN 1-85937-305-4

The Francis Frith Collection
Frith's Barn, Teffont,
Salisbury, Wiltshire SP3 5QP
Tel: +44 (0) 1722 716 376
Email: info@francisfrith.co.uk
www.francisfrith.com

Printed and bound in Great Britain

Front Cover: Bridgwater, Cornhill 1901 47866t

The colour-tinting is for illustrative purposes only, and is not intended to be historically accurate

Aerial photographs reproduced under licence from Simmons Aerofilms Limited.
Historical Ordnance Survey maps reproduced under licence from Homecheck.co.uk
Every attempt has been made to contact copyright holders of illustrative material.
We will be happy to give full acknowledgement in future editions for any items not credited.
Any information should be directed to The Francis Frith Collection.

AS WITH ANY HISTORICAL DATABASE THE FRITH ARCHIVE IS CONSTANTLY BEING
CORRECTED AND IMPROVED AND THE PUBLISHERS WOULD WELCOME INFORMATION
ON OMISSIONS OR INACCURACIES

Contents

Francis Frith: Victorian Pioneer	7
Frith's Archive - A Unique Legacy	10
Bridgwater - An Introduction	12
Around The Church	16
High Street and Penel Orlieu	22
From Cornhill to the River	34
Fore Street	43
The Bridge, Quays and Docks	48
Admiral Robert Blake	59
East of the River	64
Villages Around Bridgwater	71
Index	87
Free Mounted Print Voucher	91

Francis Frith: *Victorian Pioneer*

FRANCIS FRITH, Victorian founder of the world-famous photographic archive, was a complex and multi-talented man. A devout Quaker and a highly successful Victorian businessman, he was both philosophic by nature and pioneering in outlook.

By 1855 Francis Frith had already established a wholesale grocery business in Liverpool, and sold it for the astonishing sum of £200,000, which is the equivalent today of over £15,000,000. Now a very rich man, he was able to indulge his passion for travel. As a child he had pored over travel books written by early explorers, and his fancy and imagination had been stirred by family holidays to the sublime mountain regions of Wales and Scotland. 'What a land of spirit-stirring and enriching scenes and places!' he had written. He was to return to these scenes of grandeur in later years to 'recapture the thousands of vivid and tender memories', but with a different purpose. Now in his thirties, and captivated by the new science of photography, Frith set out on a series of pioneering journeys to the Nile regions that occupied him from 1856 until 1860.

Intrigue and Adventure

He took with him on his travels a specially-designed wicker carriage that acted as both dark-room and sleeping chamber. These far-flung journeys were packed with intrigue and adventure. In his life story, written when he was sixty-three, Frith tells of being held captive by bandits, and of fighting 'an awful midnight battle to the very point of surrender with a deadly pack of hungry, wild dogs'. Sporting flowing Arab costume, Frith arrived at Akaba by camel sixty years before Lawrence, where he encountered 'desert princes and rival sheikhs, blazing with jewel-hilted swords'.

During these extraordinary adventures he was assiduously exploring the desert regions bordering the Nile and patiently recording the antiquities and peoples with his camera. He was the first photographer to venture beyond the sixth cataract. Africa was still the mysterious 'Dark Continent', and Stanley and Livingstone's historic meeting was a decade into the future. The conditions for picture taking confound belief. He laboured for hours in his wicker dark-room in the sweltering heat of the desert, while the volatile chemicals fizzed dangerously in their trays. Often he was forced to work in remote tombs and caves where conditions were cooler. Back in London he exhibited his photographs and was 'rapturously cheered' by members of the Royal Society. His reputation as a photographer was made overnight. An eminent modern historian has likened their impact on the population of the time to that on our own generation of the first photographs taken on the surface of the moon.

Venture of a Life-Time

Characteristically, Frith quickly spotted the opportunity to create a new business as a specialist publisher of photographs. He lived in an era of immense and sometimes violent change. For the poor in the early part of Victoria's reign work was a drudge and the hours long, and people had precious little free time to enjoy themselves. Most had no transport other than a cart or gig at their disposal, and had not travelled far beyond the boundaries of their own town or village. However,

by the 1870s, the railways had threaded their way across the country, and Bank Holidays and half-day Saturdays had been made obligatory by Act of Parliament. All of a sudden the ordinary working man and his family were able to enjoy days out and see a little more of the world.

With characteristic business acumen, Francis Frith foresaw that these new tourists would enjoy having souvenirs to commemorate their days out. In 1860 he married Mary Ann Rosling and set out with the intention of photographing every city, town and village in Britain. For the next thirty years he travelled the country by train and by pony and trap, producing fine photographs of seaside resorts and beauty spots that were keenly bought by millions of Victorians. These prints were painstakingly pasted into family albums and pored over during the dark nights of winter, rekindling precious memories of summer excursions.

The Rise of Frith & Co

Frith's studio was soon supplying retail shops all over the country. To meet the demand he gathered about him a small team of photographers, and published the work of independent artist-photographers of the calibre of Roger Fenton and Francis Bedford. In order to gain some understanding of the scale of Frith's business one only has to look at the catalogue issued by Frith & Co in 1886: it runs to some 670 pages, listing not only many thousands of views of the British Isles but also many photographs of most European countries, and China, Japan, the USA and Canada – note the sample page shown opposite from the hand-written *Frith & Co* ledgers detailing pictures taken. By 1890 Frith had created the greatest specialist photographic publishing company in the

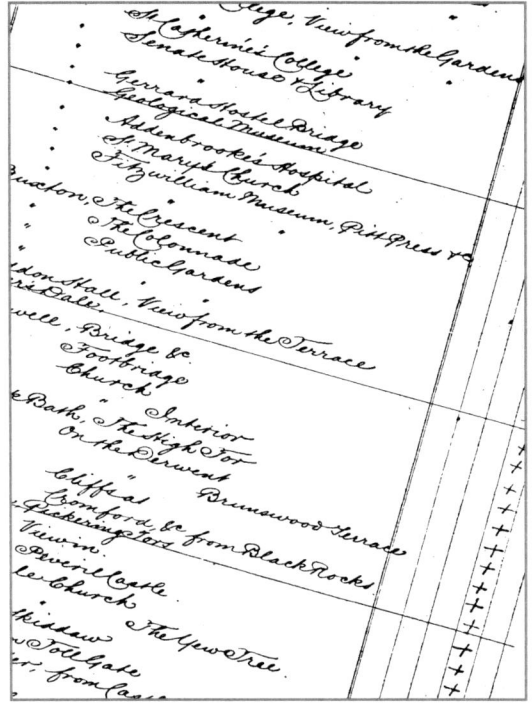

Frith's death, a new card measuring 5.5 x 3.5 inches became the standard format, but it was not until 1902 that the divided back came into being, with address and message on one face and a full-size illustration on the other. *Frith & Co* were in the vanguard of postcard development, and Frith's sons Eustace and Cyril continued their father's monumental task, expanding the number of views offered to the public and recording more and more places in Britain, as the coasts and countryside were opened up to mass travel.

Francis Frith died in 1898 at his villa in Cannes, his great project still growing. The archive he created continued in business for another seventy years. By 1970 it contained over a third of a million pictures of 7,000 cities, towns and villages. The massive photographic record Frith has left to us stands as a living monument to a special and very remarkable man.

world, with over 2,000 outlets – more than the combined number that Boots and W H Smith have today! The picture on the right shows the *Frith & Co* display board at Ingleton in the Yorkshire Dales (left of window). Beautifully constructed with a mahogany frame and gilt inserts, it could display up to a dozen local scenes.

Postcard Bonanza

The ever-popular holiday postcard we know today took many years to develop. In 1870 the Post Office issued the first plain cards, with a pre-printed stamp on one face. In 1894 they allowed other publishers' cards to be sent through the mail with an attached adhesive halfpenny stamp. Demand grew rapidly, and in 1895 a new size of postcard was permitted called the court card, but there was little room for illustration. In 1899, a year after

Frith's Archive: *A Unique Legacy*

FRANCIS FRITH'S legacy to us today is of immense significance and value, for the magnificent archive of evocative photographs he created provides a unique record of change in 7,000 cities, towns and villages throughout Britain over a century and more. Frith and his fellow studio photographers revisited locations many times down the years to update their views, compiling for us an enthralling and colourful pageant of British life and character.

We tend to think of Frith's sepia views of Britain as nostalgic, for most of us use them to conjure up memories of places in our own lives with which we have family associations. It often makes us forget that to Francis Frith they were records of daily life as it was actually being lived in the cities, towns and villages of his day. The Victorian age was one of great and often bewildering change for ordinary people, and though the pictures evoke an impression of slower times, life was as busy and hectic as it is today.

We are fortunate that Frith was a photographer of the people, dedicated to recording the minutiae of everyday life. For it is this sheer wealth of visual data, the painstaking chronicle of changes in dress, transport, street layouts, buildings, housing, engineering and landscape that captivates us so much today. His remarkable images offer us a powerful link with the past and with the lives of our ancestors.

Today's Technology

Computers have now made it possible for Frith's many thousands of images to be accessed almost instantly. In the Frith archive today, each photograph is carefully 'digitised' then stored on a CD Rom. Frith archivists can locate a single photograph amongst thousands within seconds. Views can be catalogued and sorted under a variety of categories of place and content to the immediate benefit of researchers.

Inexpensive reference prints can be created for them at the touch of a mouse button, and a wide range of books and other printed materials assembled and published for a wider, more general readership - in the next twelve months over a hundred Frith local history titles will be published! The day-to-day workings of the archive are very different from how they were in Francis Frith's time: imagine the herculean task of sorting through eleven tons of glass negatives as Frith had to do to locate a particular sequence of pictures! Yet the

See Frith at www.francisfrith.com

archive still prides itself on maintaining the same high standards of excellence laid down by Francis Frith, including the painstaking cataloguing and indexing of every view.

It is curious to reflect on how the internet now allows researchers in America and elsewhere greater instant access to the archive than Frith himself ever enjoyed. Many thousands of individual views can be called up on screen within seconds on one of the Frith internet sites, enabling people living continents away to revisit the streets of their ancestral home town, or view places in Britain where they have enjoyed holidays. Many overseas researchers welcome the chance to view special theme selections, such as transport, sports, costume and ancient monuments.

We are certain that Francis Frith would have heartily approved of these modern developments in imaging techniques, for he himself was always working at the very limits of Victorian photographic technology.

The Value of the Archive Today

Because of the benefits brought by the computer, Frith's images are increasingly studied by social historians, by researchers into genealogy and ancestory, by architects, town planners, and by teachers and schoolchildren involved in local history projects.

In addition, the archive offers every one of us an opportunity to examine the places where we and our families have lived and worked down the years. Highly successful in Frith's own era, the archive is now, a century and more on, entering a new phase of popularity.

The Past in Tune with the Future

Historians consider the Francis Frith Collection to be of prime national importance. It is the only archive of its kind remaining in private ownership and has been valued at a million pounds. However, this figure is now rapidly increasing as digital technology enables more and more people around the world to enjoy its benefits.

Francis Frith's archive is now housed in an historic timber barn in the beautiful village of Teffont in Wiltshire. Its founder would not recognize the archive office as it is today. In place of the many thousands of dusty boxes containing glass plate negatives and an all-pervading odour of photographic chemicals, there are now ranks of computer screens. He would be amazed to watch his images travelling round the world at unimaginable speeds through network and internet lines.

The archive's future is both bright and exciting. Francis Frith, with his unshakeable belief in making photographs available to the greatest number of people, would undoubtedly approve of what is being done today with his lifetime's work. His photographs, depicting our shared past, are now bringing pleasure and enlightenment to millions around the world a century and more after his death.

Bridgwater - *An Introduction*

BRIDGWATER IS A small Somerset market town. It has a wealth of history far more enticing than many casual visitors might initially expect, yet it also remains refreshingly understated.

The town, with a population of around 38,000, sits about eight miles inland from the Bristol Channel. The rolling Quantock Hills gently rise from the west while the Somerset levels, an area of wetlands, stretch out towards Glastonbury in the east. The nearest large town, Taunton, is ten miles away.

As with any town, Bridgwater has had its share of difficulties, beginning with the decline of the docks in the middle of the last century. But despite the lack of activity in the port, it has managed to emerge relatively unscathed into the 21st century.

In 1066 a Saxon, Earl Merleswain, controlled Bridgwater, which was simply called Bruggie or Bryjg (amongst many other spellings). It is said that Merleswain built the first Christian church here on the site where St Mary's now stands. With William the Conqueror's arrival, Bridgwater came under the control of Walter from Douai in France.

Since then peace and quiet have rarely featured in Bridgwater's history, but it was the medieval period that was to play one of the most important parts in its significant and colourful development.

In June 1200, King John granted his friend William de Brewer a charter, enabling him to make Bridgwater a town and fortify it with a castle. The

town sits on the lowest crossing point of the tidal River Parrett, and included in Brewer's charter were rights of lastage, whereby he could collect taxes from river traffic and control the shipping.

William de Brewer's castle and its boundaries are marked today by the river and Castle Moat on the east and west sides, Fore Street on the south, and Chandos Street to the north.

The Castle survived until the English Civil War in 1645, and few elements remain today apart from the Watergate entrance on West Quay. The last surviving parts of the castle were demolished at the beginning of the 19th century when the elegant King Square was built.

Castle Street, running down to the West Quay, dates from around 1720, and is arguably the finest street of this period in the West Country. King's Square, at the top of this street, is on the site of the old Castle, and a walk uphill from the river spans across what was the lower bailey. The level ground of Bridgwater's war memorial marks the site of the upper bailey.

There is no doubt that considerable thought has gone into recent developments to this part of the town, which have added greatly to its charm. Much of its colourful and elegant past has been retained with careful and creative attention to the contemporary style. For example, the relatively modern buildings on the northern side of the square blend in so well with the existing architecture that it takes a close inspection to tell them apart.

William Brewer also built an Augustine Priory dedicated to St John the Baptist for the benefit of the poor and infirm. Pilgrims passing through the town were welcome, with the exception of 'lunatics, lepers, and those with contagious diseases'. The hospital, known as 'The House of Augustine Friars', was at the eastern side of Eastover and gave St John's Street its name. It survived for over 300 years. In Silver Street, by St Mary's Church, stands one of the oldest doors in Somerset, which is believed to have been the gateway to a college of Greyfriars built in 1220 by William Brewer's son.

At one time Bridgwater was awash with pubs and inns, especially along the West and East Quays where the crews of ships gathered from all parts of the world. It is easy to imagine their raucous laughter coming from the old walls of the buildings. The air must have been filled with foreign and exotic languages as sailors mingled in the narrow streets.

Thus the river, with its bridge and route to the Bristol Channel, helped to transform Bridgwater from a rural market town to an important port with a wide seafaring reputation. Large, tall-masted ships would sail up to the town bridge, where the cargo would be reshipped, making Bridgwater one of the busiest maritime centres in the West of England. The town's importance as a port and trans-shipment point for sea and river traffic

remained until the beginning of the 20th century.

The 19th century witnessed a rapid period of growth in Bridgwater, and in 1841 an inner dock and tidal basin were excavated. A link was made at the western end of the dock to the Bridgwater and Taunton Canal. It was chiefly the importation of large quantities of coal by sea in the 17th century that led to the expansion of trade along the River Parrett.

Many names from the past have made their mark in and around Bridgwater, and the town's most famous son was Admiral Robert Blake. He was born in August 1599 and died in 1657 at sea near Plymouth. His statue stands in front of the market hall (built in 1826) in Cornhill, the medieval market place. The house where Robert Blake was born, in Blake Street, is now a museum and contains many relics of his life.

In 1685 the Monmouth Rebellion came to Bridgwater and the Duke of Monmouth, illegitimate son of Charles II and Lucy Walters, was proclaimed King of England on Cornhill. On 6 July 1685, he led his troops, the infamous pitchfork army, into the brutal battle at nearby Sedgemoor, the last one to be fought on English soil. This ended in defeat and he was later beheaded in the Tower of London. The ruthless actions of Judge Jeffreys, despatched by King James to sort out the rebels, leave behind far less affectionate memories. Even now, particularly on summer nights, it is said that sounds of horses' hooves and wailing cries from the wounded can be heard coming across the moorland. It is reputed that Monmouth himself has been seen galloping over the countryside and these sightings, along with many other legends that surround those tragic events, have spanned the centuries.

George Williams, knighted in 1894, was the founder of the YMCA. While living and working in Bridgwater he became a devout Christian and developed the idea of a Young Mans Christian Association. He opened the first branch in 1844 and the Bridgwater branch in 1859. The organisation became one of the largest in the world and the George Williams memorial hall was built in 1887. It stood next to the bridge, on the corner of Eastover and Salmon Parade.

Market days in Bridgwater are a long serving tradition dating back to medieval times, and originally there were two crosses. The High Cross was on the Cornhill site from the 14th century until it was pulled down in 1827, and St Mary's Cross, originally at the corner of the churchyard, was moved to Penel Orlieu in 1769 and finally demolished in 1830. While the circular base can still be seen in the churchyard, a replica also stands at the riverside end of Fore Street.

A variety of traders would flock to the town on market days, especially those associated with the cloth and wool industry. Flemish weavers brought the woollen trade to Somerset in the 14th century.

As late as the middle of the last century the markets would cause quite a stir, with cattle being driven through the streets and sheep meandering across the bridge. Horses were tied up all along the river and people from the surrounding villages would arrive laden with butter, cream, eggs and cheeses. Later in the evening they would leave, with their traps full of other wares. To many country folk, these were days of great excitement, as well as the main opportunity to sell their wares.

A popular event was the annual Bridgwater Fair, held in September on St Matthew's field, to the west of the town. It lasted for four days and dates back to the 17th century. There was also a thriving trade in human labour. Carters, shepherds and milkmaids would line up in rows, wielding their whips, crooks or stools as they waited to be chosen for their particular skills. Entertainment was always a major part of these fairs, including fighting gypsies, striptease tents and travelling theatres. Needless to say, the pubs did a roaring trade and a good time was had by all.

Bridgwater Carnival has also played a significant part in the town's activities, and continues to this day. It traditionally originates from the Gunpowder Plot, and is the first and biggest of the Somerset winter carnivals. It takes place in early November, with a procession of more than a hundred illuminated floats making their way through the town centre. A large bonfire was lit on the Cornhill, but this practice had to stop in 1924 when the roads in the town were laid with tarmac. But undaunted the Carnival continues and the costumes and floats become more elaborate and extravagant year by year. Carnival 'gangs', usually based in local pubs and clubs compete with each other for the best float.

In the 18th and 19th centuries, Bridgwater developed as a small but productive industrial centre producing bricks, tiles and glass. Its chief industry during Victorian days was the manufacture of 'Bath Bricks', made from sand and clay deposited by the tides of the river. These products were exported from the town by various means, involving the canal and docks and subsequently the railway. On the lower bank of the River Parrett, the chimneys of the former Barhams Brickworks were a significant landmark. Now all that remains is one brick kiln, which was restored by the County Council in 1991 to form the basis of the Somerset Brick and Tile Museum. After the Second World War, the Council acquired the docks to ensure their preservation, and today the area has been redeveloped for housing and a marina. Wares Warehouse has been converted into flats, a pub and a restaurant.

In the 1930's British Cellophane brought new industry into Bridgwater, employing much of the town's workforce and making a major contribution to the local economy. Along with this new source of jobs came a distinct and unpleasant smell created by the manufacturing process, which has since been cured by new methods.

Hidden away behind the Angel Crescent Shopping Centre is a modest cluster of little restaurants and small cafés, an ideal spot for sampling West Country fare and resting weary feet. For those who prefer something stronger, plenty of inns and pubs can be reached within crawling distance.

This book sets out to show Bridgwater as our parents and grandparents would have seen it, and hopefully this compilation of photographs will take the reader on a nostalgic journey into the past.

Around The Church

Somerset has an outstanding collection of church towers, standing in all their glory whether they are on the sharp hill slopes of the Quantocks, across the great expanse of fenland or as the focal point of a town. St Mary's Church is no exception, and is an ideal starting point for exploring Bridgwater. It is perpendicular in style, and there are also traces of Norman and medieval architecture. It is thought that there was once a Saxon church on the site, which served the pre-town settlement. The rose window above the north door has canopied recesses, decorated with hearts, diamonds, clubs and spades. The red stone tower and octagonal spire has looked down on life in Bridgwater for six centuries, while the weathercock surveys the surrounding marshlands from its grand height of 175 feet.

St Mary's Church 1890 24897
The tall slim spire appears to dwarf this group of youngsters as they pose with their penny-farthing. The steeple was badly damaged by lightning during a terrific thunderstorm in 1813. Sixty-five years later the church was closed for six months while the pillars and arches were scraped and cleaned.

Around The Church

St Mary's Church 1906 55773
Although the street was empty at the time of this photograph, it must have had plenty of horse-drawn traffic a little earlier, judging by the mess on the road. Sadly the superb railings around the Church grounds have long gone, apart from the gate and one small section to the left of the view.

St Mary's Church 1906 55774
On the eve of the Battle of Sedgemoor the Duke of Monmouth climbed to the top of this tower. From here, he could survey the countryside and see for himself the position of the King's troops before he left for his final battle.

St Mary's Church, The Altar 1906 55776
This late Renaissance altar painting, "Descent from the Cross", was believed to have been acquired in a sale of naval prizes at Plymouth in the 18th century and presented to the town by Lord Anne Poulett, who was inconsiderately named after his godmother, Queen Anne. John the Baptist leans over the body of Christ, with the Virgin Mary collapsed in the arms of Mary Magdalene.

Around The Church

St Mary's Street 1913 65366
The higgledy-piggledy coming together of ages and styles adds to the timeless charm of this quiet part of the street. The petrol pump swing arms belonging to the garage on the right hang in vain towards a road empty of traffic. Above them, Western Gas displays a bold advertisement.

Marycourt House c1890 B205501
The ground floor of this carved oak fronted house is now a shop and restaurant. The Elizabethan windows have sadly gone and the façade has been altered, although the first floor remains virtually unchanged.

▼ Marycourt House 1913 65367

Judge Jeffreys is reputed to have stayed here when on his mission to sort out the rebels during his notorious bloody assizes. Just around the corner at the Cornhill, many of the Duke of Monmouth's ill-fated followers were hanged, drawn and quartered.

▼ St Mary's Church 1936 87457

A few minor intrusions of the present day, like the occasional motorcar and inevitable road markings, make little impression on this scene, which has scarcely changed in the past three hundred years. The oldest grave in the church grounds is that of James Hartnell, who died in 1866 at the good age of 102.

▲ St Mary's Street c1955
B205072

The Rose & Crown Inn dates back to the 14th century, while the Tudor Café, now a hotel, dates from around 1600. These and Marycourt house, opposite the church, are some of the oldest buildings in the town. The street remains relatively unchanged today.

Around The Church

◀ **St Mary's Street c1965**
B205116
The Crofton Hotel on the right remains, and A & S White is now the Friarn Court Hotel. The tall building to the centre-left of the view has gone. Scooters add to the rapidly increasing volume of traffic.

High Street and Penel Orlieu

Originally there was an 'Island' of narrow buildings running along the middle of the High Street, which in effect made two narrow streets. As new buildings went up, the building line was moved forward several feet and the Island disappeared altogether in 1856, when the remaining buildings were demolished.

Royal Clarence Hotel 1890 27901
The Royal Clarence Hotel's porch bears a plaque with the initials of Robert Codington, the Bridgwater Corporation's Arms and the year 1795. This plaque was originally in the centre of the span of the Town Bridge, and along with many other souvenirs from the old bridge, was sold to cover the costs of the new one opened in 1883.

High Street 1902 48713
The Georgian-style building on the left is the Town Hall and was opened in 1823. It now bears a plaque commemorating a visit by the Queen on 8 May 1987. The building next door, beyond the two lamps, is occupied by Sedgemoor District Council's Housing Department and now has a balcony. The boys in their breeches are captivated by the photographer, while the group on the right pose before an impressive display of hats.

High Street 1913 65364
This and the following two pictures are all taken from a similar spot and span a total of thirty-seven years, during which many changes have taken place. By 1936 the gas lamps have been removed and there is no longer a cab rank in the middle of the road.

High Street 1936 87455
Twenty-three years later and cars begin to line the streets. The Golden Ball hotel down on the left is now Holts public house. In February 1855, a severe snow and sleet storm visited the town and severe losses were sustained. Mr James Leaker, proprietor of the Golden Ball, had 2,000 bushels of malt ruined, which would have made a lot of beer.

High Street c1950
B205016
Buses and lorries now add to the increasing traffic. The gas board sign in the centre covers an original W H Smith sign, which today is exposed once again. The shop below is now a bookshop, and if you stand underneath the sign you get a good view of St Mary's spire looming ahead.

St Mary's Church Spire 1936 87456
This view remains remarkably unchanged and can be seen while standing in Mansion House Lane, behind the Mansion House Pub on the corner of the High Street. The white building underneath the church is the White Lion.

High Street c1950 B205036
The Royal Clarence (on the right) was built in Regency style in 1825 on the site of two former inns, the Crown at the front, facing Cornhill, and the Angel at the rear, from which the shopping centre now takes its name. It was also once known as Longhurst's Hotel in 1865 after the proprietor at that time, and in 1866 a Mr Leaker, previously of the Golden Ball Hotel, took over.

Penel Orlieu and High Street c1960 B205069
This street was originally the junction of Pynel Street and Orlieu Street (now Clare Street) and during Queen Victoria's reign it had its fair share of taverns and inns in support of the regular cattle markets held there since 1875. The Queen in the centre was sometimes referred to as the Round House and the Market House Inn towards High Street (on the left of the view) is now the Valiant Soldier. F Turner and son, on the left, is now the home of the Governing Council of the Cat Fancy.

▼ **High Street c1955** B205071
B E Radfords, on the left, is now the entrance to Angel Place Shopping Centre. Bristol Hotel is now Barclays Bank, and the pretty canopies over the entrance have long gone. The tall building at the end of the street has gone, and the Post Office stands in its place. Its neighbour, now Lloyds TSB, holds a plaque celebrating the last Cornhill Bonfire in 1924.

▼ **Penel Orlieu c1960** B205070
We are standing with the High Street behind us. Rowntrees are making a delivery to the Odeon cinema, currently showing 'Genevieve'. Opened in 1936, it stands on the site of the cattle market and is now a Mecca Bingo Hall. Bert Beavers Tailor's shop is now a bar.

▲ **North Street c1960**
B205079
This is one of the oldest streets in the town. The buildings on the left remain, and so does the Malt Shovel Inn at the end, which was pulled down and rebuilt in 1904. Meaker's Motors on the right, now the Bridgwater Ford Garage, was once Miss Everdale's school for girls.

High Street and Penel Orlieu

◄ **Broadway Lido c1960**
B205094
This sparkling, newly opened lido gave the town its long-awaited swimming baths but was demolished a few years ago to make way for a new Safeway store. The rooftops to the left can still be seen from the supermarket's car park.

Castle Street 1894 34848
Shadows lengthen across this elegant Georgian street, easily recognisable more than one hundred years after this picture was taken. Uphill from the river, it reaches Kings Square and the Bridgwater War Memorial at the top. Built in 1723 by the first Duke of Chandos, it was originally known as Chandos Street. Towards the top on the right is the Mary Stanley House and opposite is the Bridgwater Arts Centre, the first in the country.

The War Memorial Gardens 1927 80590
This memorial, erected in 1924 to commemorate the dead of the First World War, stands in the centre of Kings Square. It features a mother and child, and represents civilisation. The square is now surrounded by seats and is a popular place for taking the sun.

King Square c1950 B205013
The Employment Exchange building in the centre was once Miss Johnson's School for boys and girls. Railings with entrance gates surrounded the gardens, where the pupils took their exercise. Many of the smart houses had cellars, balconies and shutters on the windows. New buildings in the vernacular style have been erected on the left, and once again railings enclose the gardens.

From Cornhill to the River

Although it is merely a hop and a skip from the church, plenty of time can be spent absorbing the history surrounding Cornhill and the Market place, which today continues to be the very heart of the town. The Market House and Dome were built in 1826. Since then they have seen many elaborate celebrations, including the unveiling of Admiral Robert Blake's statue in 1900. In 1605, with the failure of the Gunpowder Plot, Bridgwater, along with other towns and villages, celebrated with the traditional bonfire and fireworks display. But in Bridgwater this tradition was to develop into what has now become the world's largest night-time carnival. The bonfire was the centrepiece at Cornhill until 1924, when tarmac was introduced on the roads.

The Market and Church 1890 27899
Beneath the shadows of St Mary's spire, children play in the traffic-free market place while horses wait patiently. The Market House, now generally known as the Dome, is the heart of the town, where Cornhill and Fore Street meet. The pineapple on top of the dome is a symbol of welcome. The railings around the market were necessary to keep the sheep and cattle from upsetting the traders' stalls.

The Market House 1897 40000
Seven years later and the railings have gone, having been removed in 1895. In the year of this photograph, civic dignitaries and townspeople gathered to give thanks for Queen Victoria's Diamond Jubilee. The Bristol Arms Hotel building on the right is now a Barclays Bank, and Dyer's Dining Rooms on the left of the dome now serve as public conveniences.

The Blake Statue 1901 46321
Along with the Cornhill behind it, Blake's statue is Bridgwater's best-known landmark. Built in hollow bronze in 1900, it cost £1,200 and was paid for by contribution from the Victorian public. It remains an ideal meeting point to stop and discuss the bargains of the day.

Cornhill 1901 47866
The unhurried pace in this scene appears to have been adopted by all, apart from the grey horses who look as if they're eager to be on their way! The Lipton sign on the building to the left has disappeared, but Impeys Stores continues to be a confectioner.

Blake's Statue 1901 47868
This was a favourite spot to sit and watch the Edwardian world go by; maybe the unusual sight of the photographer has stopped all these people in their tracks. Note the smart fashions of the day, as modelled by the boy and girl to the right of Admiral Blake.

The Market and the Royal Clarence Hotel 1902 48709
The Royal Clarence Hotel was called The Royal Hotel until the Duke of Clarence (later William the Fourth) was passing through and stopped there to change horses. The year of this photograph saw Edward VII's coronation and the end of the Boer War, and the Cornhill was the centre of elaborate celebrations for both events.

Cornhill c1950 B205041
Half a century later, and the pace of life has increased. There are now many new signs and posts jostling for space. Maynard's Restaurant to the right of the Dome has always remained an eating-place despite numerous changes in ownership, and today it belongs to Kentucky Fried Chicken.

The Cornhill c1955
B205018
The rain persists and a long queue is being formed as shoppers huddle underneath the bus shelter. This view is taken from the opposite side of the Market Place, standing on the corner of Fore Street.

The Cornhill c1950 B205015
The rain hasn't dampened these shoppers' post-war optimism as they gather round the Market square in their hunt for bargains. At the time of this picture the Post Office was in the Market Hall, so perhaps the caped gentleman crossing the road is a postman.

Blake's Memorial c1955 B205034
Today Admiral Blake stands further down Fore Street to make room for the pedestrianisation and seating, although he continues to cast an impressive shadow across the market place. The handcart appears to be laden with bargains.

Fore Street

In medieval times this street was known simply as "Between Church and Bridge" and remains the same narrow width today as it winds its way downhill from the Cornhill towards the river. Fore Street was once the home of the old police station and town gaol until it was moved to the High Street in 1875, and then to Northgate in 1911. In its Fore Street days, the local police force amounted to less than a dozen to maintain law and order in the town, and policemen carried canes to use on troublesome youngsters.

View from the Cornhill 1890 27900
The delightful sign and lanterns of Hill haberdashery have been removed and the shop is now Burtons Menswear, while Edinburgh Wool Shop occupies John Whitby & Sons' Art Materials. The Dining Rooms sign above Rich watchmakers belonged to its predecessor King & Son. The sign has since disappeared and a travel agent occupies the site. Street traders move freely along the empty road.

Fore Street 1913
65365
We are standing in the shelter of the Market Place, looking towards Fore Street. The Provincial Bank of England building to the left of Admiral Blake still stands, but is now a charity shop. Between the pillars on the left, the pony and trap are outside Oliver's Boots and Shoes, one of the early chain stores and a sign of the new trend in modern life.

Fore Street

◀ **Fore Street 1902**
48711
By 1913 the Home & Colonial Stores building had been replaced by Marks & Spencer, although they no longer remain there. This building, along with its neighbours, was once the site of the castle moat. The motorcar was a rare sight in 1902 and the horse rider looks to be moving out of its way.

▼ **Fore Street c1950**
B205043
This view is looking away from the bridge, towards Cornhill. The Worlds store on the right was previously the Golden Key stores and is now Key Markets. On the other side of the road was the site of the old Bridgwater Gaol. The building was pulled down in 1930.

◀ **The Cornhill c1955**
B205087
This panoramic view of the spire, the Cornhill and the dome sees very little traffic making use of the smart new road lay out. It is a bright, sunny day with blinds over the shop fronts and hanging baskets around the Dome. Peacetime prosperity begins to show its mark.

▼ **Fore Street c1955** B205063
The serpents' heads bursting forth on the chimney on the right can still be found. The Fore Street Clothing Co. building was once the site of the Castle Inn, a famous hostelry of seafaring men in Victorian days. The building was demolished in the late 1960s and the Nationwide Building Society now occupies the site.

▼ **Fore Street c1955** B205078
The Marks and Spencer building on the left is easily recognisable with its familiar architecture and logo. Bold lettering and big, brash signs of the time begin to replace the individual sign writing of previous years.

▲ **Fore Street c1955**
B205042
An early Freeman Hardy Willis with its glass plate shop front occupies the building to the left, and further along is the site of the former Bridgwater Mercury offices, which tragically burnt down in 1883, claiming the lives of the editor's wife and three daughters.

Fore Street

◀ **Fore Street c1955** B205060
The larger chain stores begin to make their presence known with the arrival of Olivers, Boots, Frisbys and Burton. The Earncombe Hairdresser sign has been removed and the Circulating Library is now NEXT. In 1865 the premises belonged to Mr Archibald Graham, stationer and bookseller.

The Bridge, Quays and Docks

No visit to Bridgwater would be complete without spending time by the River Parrett, taking a walk along the towpath towards the Docks, and visiting the quiet waters of the Bridgwater and Taunton Canal. The town bridge has witnessed countless events, including the river freezing over in the winter of 1895. Bonfires were lit below the bridge and the townspeople gathered to enjoy an ox roast, but it cannot be forgotten that the severe conditions also caused great distress and many soup kitchens were opened.

YMCA and the Bridge 1890 27897
The original town bridge was medieval and in 1795 was replaced by a single span cast iron bridge of a 'curious mechanism' made at Coalbrookdale. This survived for almost ninety years until it was found to be too steep for the changing traffic demands and was replaced with great pomp and ceremony in 1883.

The Bridge, Quays and Docks

View Across the Bridge 1890 27898
Here we are looking along Fore Street, with a fine view of Cornhill. St Mary's spire sits amongst the chimneys. The pub in the centre is now Bristol and West Building Society. A lone horse drawn wagon crosses the bridge while some activity in the river is attracting everyone's attention.

The Bridge c1960 B205093
In 1883 the Lady Mayor undertook the new bridge's opening ceremony because her husband was ill. But the story says that when she arrived home, she found he was perfectly well and had spent a pleasant afternoon with his mistress. That year's carnival procession used the bridge for the first time.

The Bridge, Quays and Docks

The Bridge 1902
48712
The large YMCA building, now demolished, was originally the site of the Globe Hotel, which burnt down in 1875. York House on the opposite corner still stands. Eastover has been decorated with flags and bunting, perhaps for one of the two memorable events of the year, Edward the Seventh's Coronation or the end of the Boer War. The small buildings in front of the YMCA building are toilet blocks, built in 1868.

◀ **The Bridge 1903** 50451
This Edwardian scene looks downstream, with the West Quay to the left, once lined with ships loading and unloading cargo from many corners of the world. During the course of that year 2,976 ships entered the port carrying a total of 163,960 tons. Coal was landed from South Wales and ships left Bridgwater laden with bricks, tiles and textiles.

The Bridge, Quays and Docks

◀ **The Bridge 1902** 48710
The Dutch-like high gable on the Wilkinson building is a reminder of the presence of Flemish weavers during the development of the woollen trade in the 14th century. Today the building remains largely unchanged, but the lettering has been removed. The Punch Bowl Inn next door closed in 1964 and was replaced by a building society.

▼ **The River 1927** 80592
This tranquil scene of the muddy tidal waters of the River Parrett shows a family sitting on the riverbank at high tide and enjoying the views across Blake Gardens. Although this particular day looks sunny, there was a terrific thunderstorm in July of this year and several parts of the town were flooded.

◀ **The Lions 1894** 34849
Once one of the finest houses in Bridgwater, this was built around 1720 by Benjamin Holloway. He was the builder commissioned by James Bridge (first Duke of Chandos) to construct Castle Street. The lions on the gateposts might actually be Chinese style dogs. This entire scene remains unchanged, apart from the disappearance of the pineapples above the door and some alterations to the roof.

Francis Frith's Around Bridgwater

The Bridge, Quays and Docks

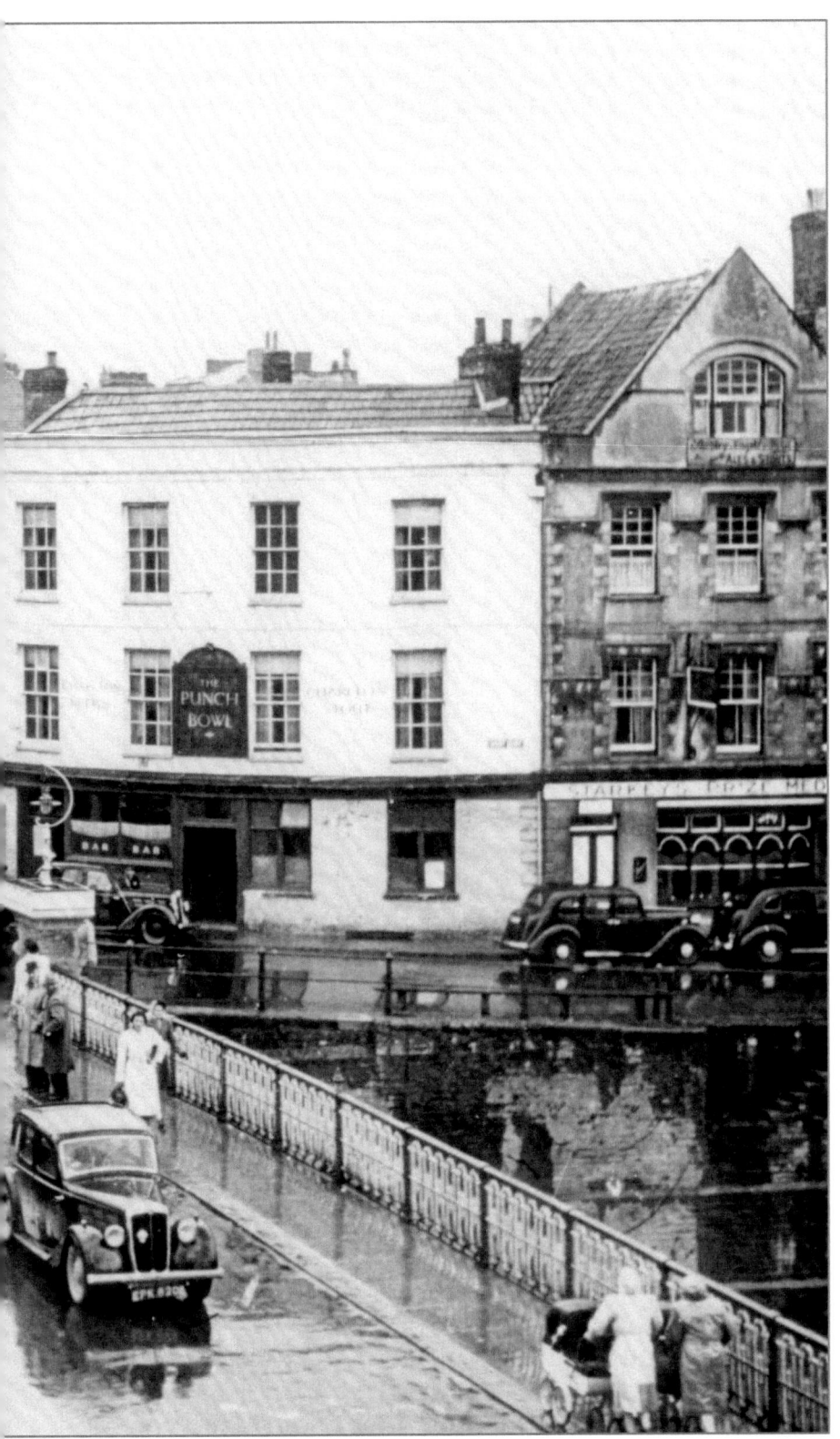

The Bridge c1950
B205023
Horse brake outings were a regular event from the Punch Bowl Inn and day-trippers would set off for the country or seaside. The electric lamps on the bridge have since been removed and the recent installation of replica streetlamps is a welcome improvement.

West Quay c1950 B205029
The first building on the left was originally the site of the Anchor Inn, another favourite with sailors, but in 1911 was taken over by the Odd Fellows in the town. It is now Fisherman's Wharf. Alongside the Watergate Hotel, to the right of the view between Castle Street and Chandos Street, the stone arch of the Watergate can still be seen, where supplies were delivered from the river to the castle.

The Bridge, Quays and Docks

◀ The River and Bridge 1897 39998
Sea going vessels once crowded the banks of the river. A vessel is in the dry dock of Carver & Sons, and the dock entrance on the left is where the bus station now stands. The dry dock fell into disuse and filled with water, but was subsequently filled-in following a tragic drowning accident around the time of this picture. The staging has gone, but today there are still some moorings on the right.

▼ West Quay c1955
B205050
Long gone are the tangles of rigging that used to line the quays. So too are the days when the taverns were filled with local mariners and seafarers from all over the world. Starkey Knight & Ford finally closed down in 1964 and is now part of Whitbread. The demise of the Northgate brewery and its prize ales was a matter of great regret to the locals.

◀ West Quay c1955
B205062
The views along the river have now changed considerably, partly because the river walls have been raised. At one time, the top of the bank was level with the road and flooding was a regular occurrence. The chimney and all but one of the brick kilns have now been demolished, and this stands as a fitting memorial to Bridgwater's industrial past.

The Town Bridge c1960 B205084
The centre building on the right is Wilkinson & Leng, Builders' Merchants. It was previously Harwood's Timber and Slate Mills and the old Post Office was next door until 1909. The last ship built at Bridgwater, the 'Irene', was launched here in 1907.

The Docks 1927 80593
We are looking across the docks from the entrance lock to the canal. The decline and closure of these docks has prompted a marina development and today the scene is significantly quieter. The building in the centre is now the only reminder of the dock's earlier importance.

Victoria Road Bridge 1936 87459
This bridge, opened on 22 October 1931, crosses the Bridgwater and Taunton Canal. It was built by E. Ireland. The canal was once an important trading link to Taunton and many other inland places, but now the shadows across its waters are rarely disturbed.

Admiral Robert Blake

Although he was one of Bridgwater's most famous sons, it was not until 1900 that Admiral Blake's statue was erected on the Cornhill, while forty-five years later a plaque in his memory was laid in Westminster Abbey. But today many tributes to his brilliant naval career can be found around the town, including the Commonwealth flag, which continues to fly over his house.

Binford House 1900 46314
Until it was demolished in 1905 to provide the site for a new public library, Binford House with its riverside gardens was the home of Richard Else, the co-designer of the Town Bridge. Behind it, in Binford Place, stands St Joseph's Roman Catholic Church, built in 1882.

Blake Gardens Avenue 1900 46318
Situated in tranquillity a few minutes' walk from the bustle of the town centre, this was a popular chestnut walk and the subject of many postcards. When this view was taken, Binford House would have been on the left. The trees lean towards the river on the right.

Blake Gardens 1906 55769
The photographer seems to have captured everyone's attention, including the three lads standing by the decorated gothic archway. The little girls make a striking picture in their Edwardian outfits, and the new library can be seen in between the trees on the right.

Blake Gardens 1902 48715
Binford House conservatory is peeking through the trees on the left. Neither the house nor the two structures still stand, the central flowerbed has gone and six years after this photograph was taken, a bandstand was added.

The Public Library c1965 B205118
The official opening ceremony was performed in 1906, the foundation stone having been laid 11 months earlier. The library, with its pillared porch, is an Edwardian variation of the Cornhill building. It cost £3,500 to build and was funded with an endowment by Andrew Carnegie. The first librarian earned £75 a year, but to compare, in 1906 Whisky was 3s 2d a bottle and sausages 7d a lb!

Blake's Birth Place 1906 55771
Opened in 1926 as the Admiral Blake museum, the house holds collections of local and maritime history, with particular features of the 17th century and the Monmouth Rebellion of 1685. The building at the end has now gone, but the little archway is still there.

Blake's Birth Place 1906 55770
It is unlikely that Robert Blake would recognise this house, where he was born in 1599. Although it still stands, it had been much changed by 1906. The lower half of the stucco has since been removed, exposing the original walling and neither the original door or windows remain. Yet, somehow, this quiet little street still manages to retain some of the 16th-century atmosphere.

Francis Frith's Around Bridgwater

East of the River

Leaving Fore Street and crossing the town bridge will take us into Eastover, on the east bank of the river.

Eastover c1950 B205031
The building beyond the Ship Aground Hotel belonged to Waddon & Sons, Ironmongers, who first began trading in the town as rope-makers. Woolworth's now occupies the building to the left and the countless examples of tobacco advertisements would now be illegal.

Eastover c1950 B205030
The buildings of the tobacconists and furnishers to the immediate left in this view are no longer standing, and the site now belongs to the Eastgate Bridgwater Community Church.

Eastover c1955 B205051
The busy streets reflect the rapid development of new housing in the area. Shoppers are engrossed with their business, but the two little girls on the right have found the time to stop and enjoy their moment of fame. The motorbike and sidecar look particularly uncomfortable.

Eastover c1955 B205075
Today this view is barely recognisable, apart from the buildings fronting West Quay, which can be spotted in the distance. The Devonshire Arms, home to one of the many Bridgwater Carnival clubs, closed in 1963, and the little Arcade cinema next door, opened in 1929, finally gave way to the larger complex in Penel Orlieu.

St John Street c1955 B205054
This street owes its development to the railway, which arrived in 1841. Originally it was the site of the medieval Hospital of St John, which lasted until the dissolution of the monasteries in the 16th century. The Baker's Arms is now Rebels Retreat, and the building beyond it was once the Mariner's Congregational Church, built in 1837 for the use of seamen. It now stands empty downstairs, with flats above.

Monmouth Street c1950 B205033
It is difficult to imagine that this was the site of the horse fairs held in the early part of the twentieth century, and although the Mills building still stands today, most of this scene has once again changed beyond all recognition.

Blake Bridge c1960 B205091
Opened in 1958, this bridge was built on the site of the old wooden Lime Bridge, and was part of the traffic scheme to reduce bottlenecks in the town centre. Before then, the Town Bridge was the only road bridge over the Parrett. Hundreds of people attended the ceremony, including some who had seen the opening of the Town Bridge 75 years before. The trees beyond the bridge, to the right of the picture, border the Public Library and Blake Gardens.

Villages Around Bridgwater

The villages featured in this book, as delightful as their names suggest, all sit within 10 miles of Bridgwater in some of England's most unforgettable countryside. The landscape, rich with mysteries and legends, is a blend of hills, moors and marshes to three sides, while the fourth boundary stretches out to the waters of Bridgwater Bay.

High Ham, The Village c1965 H508010
Standing 500 feet up with a wide view of the hills, High Ham has been mellowed by centuries and remains unspoiled. Although the Kings Head still stands, the house on the left has now gone, and gardens to a new house front the road. There is far more to the village than this view suggests.

Othery, The Village c1960 0102018
The village stands high on a ridge in the centre of Sedgemoor, and was once called Zoyland. The cottages huddle together beyond the reach of floods, overlooking an expanse of fenland, broken by a few isolated low hills. Pollard willows provided the raw material for the village's basket industries.

Othery, The London Inn c1960 0102004
The London Inn still stands and is easily recognisable, so too is the view, which remains much the same. Othery village school is to the right, with the church beyond it.

Middlezoy, The Village c1960 M372010
Although the house and view remains, the sold sign on the right is now the site of bungalows. Some of the Royalist soldiers from the Battle of Sedgemoor were billeted in the village's 600 year-old church.

Westonzoyland, General View c1960 W603014
Ghostly memories of the Battle of Sedgemoor are preserved for evermore in the ancient church, whose yellow-grey tower is a superb landmark in the flat landscape. Many wounded prisoners were locked up here until daybreak. Five died in the church and the survivors were later herded to Bridgwater, although some were hanged on route. A memorial marks the site of the battle beside a ditch canal at the edge of the village.

East Lyng, The Rose and Crown c1960 E239009
This street remains easily recognisable, although Starkey's Prize Ales are no longer brewed and the pub is now a free house. The village's small church was originally a chapel. King Alfred built it in recognition of the shelter given to him at nearby Athelney during his fight with the Danes.

East Lyng, The Village c1960 E239010
Looking with the pub now behind us, the view continues to be mostly unchanged, although the first building on the left, Whitehead General Stores, is now a house. The magnificent yews outside what is appropriately named Yew Tree House are sadly no longer there.

Kingston St Mary, The Village c1960 K179008
Almost nothing has changed on this sleepy little Somerset corner and, unusually, the village shop on the left remains. The second building on the right is part of Alpha Cottages, now a pretty whitewashed row with enchanting little gardens. The building beyond is the pub.

Wembdon, St George's Church 1894 34856
The 15th century was a time of great prosperity for Wembdon, when claims of miraculous cures from a local well brought large numbers of pilgrims to the church. Destroyed by fire in 1867, it was subsequently rebuilt in 1870 and not long after the photograph a vestry was added. Otherwise, it looks much the same today.

Nether Stowey, Castle Street 1895
35764
Crowded with little houses on tiny streets, the village is set in the foothills of the Quantocks. The gentle ripple of the stream running down from the Mount breaks the silence in this quiet little street. The Mount is the highest part of the village and is the site of an 11th-century motte and bailey castle. It has magnificent views across Bridgwater Bay to the Welsh Mountains.

Francis Frith's Around Bridgwater

**Nether Stowey,
St Mary's Street 1929**
82113
The stream continues to flow down through the village, which apart from the inevitable parked cars looks very much the same today. Samuel Coleridge's cottage, where he lived and entertained his literary friends Wordsworth and Lamb, is in the far distance on the left and is now owned by the National Trust.

Nether Stowey, Post Office and Clock Tower 1929 82138
The bell from the former market cross was used for the Clock Tower. It was erected to commemorate Queen Victoria's Silver Jubilee, with the faces installed to mark her Diamond in 1897. Since then, the centenary of Parish Councils in 1997 has been marked with yet another face. This was also the site of the village lock-up and stocks.

Holford, The Triscombe Stone 1898 40347
The stone marks an ancient meeting point of drovers' tracks, used since the Bronze Age. Quietness may be awarded by a sighting of a buzzard, kestrel or meadow pipit. Badgers can also be seen at dusk, although it is said that on certain dark nights beasts from the Otherworld, known as the Yeth Hounds, run loose.

Cannington, The Village c1965
C733020

Translated from Old English, the name means 'The King's Enclosure'. The Blue Anchor to the left of the view is now the Friendly Spirit, while Libby stores is a house. Brook Lane to the right of the pub leads to the old vicarage and the church, whose spire is no longer hidden by trees.

Holford, Alfoxton House 1903 50458

In 1797 William Wordsworth and his sister Dorothy rented this magnificent Queen Anne house on the slopes of the Quantock Hills. They regularly entertained friends, including Samuel Taylor Coleridge from nearby Nether Stowey, and for hours would wander over the hills and down into the glens. But their strange accents and wild talk of the French Revolution caused suspicion with the locals and renewal of the lease was subsequently refused. The house is now a hotel.

Dunball c1960 P384014

If the Poplar trees lining the A38 had suffered the same fate as the trees in the foreground, this view would be difficult to find today. The railway sidings are gone, and the motorway cuts through the foreground of what is now mostly industrial development. The wharf in the distance is on a bend of the river Parrett and is marked by cranes. It remains in use today with ships unloading granite, sand and other cargoes.

▼ **Pawlett, The Crooked Chimney Restaurant c1960** P382504
Safe on high ground, the village with its lush grazing pastures stretching out towards the sea once belonged to John of Gaunt. Unfortunately, the restaurant here was demolished in the early 1990s to make room for a development that never happened.

▼ **Huntspill, The Village 1903** 50178
Twenty-eight people died in this village in 1606 because the sea broke its bank at nearby Burnham. 'Pill' means tidal creek in Celtic. The Methodist Church has lost its railings, but the pub on the left further down, still serves the village. While the buildings in this view have suffered no dramatic changes, it is difficult to imagine that this was the main Bridgwater to Bristol road.

▲ **Puriton, The Crossroads c1960**
P384018
Salt mining was a local industry until the beginning of the 20th century. This cottage still stands, and remains a corner shop with an off licence, although the façade has been considerably altered and the tobacco advertisements are no longer a familiar sight.

Villages Around Bridgwater

◀ **Woolavington, General View c1960**
W595009
This village lies on the slopes of the Polden Hills, with views across the flat dykeland that stretches away to Burnham. Looking down Woolavington Hill, the road is on the right and the field is now a housing development. The church can still be seen beyond the roofs of the houses, and the white house at the bottom is featured in the view over the page.

**Woolavington,
The Post Office c1960** W595014

As is common in so many villages, the post office has moved more than once in recent years, and is now situated in a substantial housing development at the top of the hill near where a windmill once stood. Woolavington was once part of the manor of Shapwick, which was owned by the Abbott of Glastonbury.

Index

Bridgwater

Binford House 59
Blake's Birth Place 62, 63
Blake Gardens 60, 61
Blake's Statue 35, 38, 42
The Bridge 48, 49, 50-51, 52-53, 54-55,
           56-57, 58
Broadway Lido 31
Castle Street 32
Cornhill 36-37, 39, 40-41, 42, 43, 45
The Docks 58
Eastover 64-65, 66, 67
High Street 24, 25, 26-27, 29, 30
Fore Street 44-45, 46-47
King Square 33
Lake Bridge 70
The Lions 53
The Market 34, 39
Market House 35
Marycourt House 19, 20
Monmouth Street 68-69
North Street 30-31
Penel Orlieu 29, 30
Public Library 62
The River 53, 56-57

Royal Clarence Hotel 22-23, 39
St Mary's Church 16, 17, 18, 20, 28, 34
St Mary's Street 19, 20-21
St John Street 67
Victoria Road Bridge 58
War Memorial 32
West Quay 56, 57

Around and About

Cannington 82-83
Dunball 83
East Lyng 74
High Ham 71
Holford 82-83
Huntspill 84
Kingston St Mary 75
Middlezoy 73
Nether Stowey 76-77, 78-79, 80-81
Othery 72
Pawcett 84
Puriton 84-85
Wembdon 75
Westonzoyland 73
Woolavington 85, 86

FRITH PRODUCTS & SERVICES

Francis Frith would doubtless be pleased to know that the pioneering publishing venture he started in 1860 still continues today. Over a hundred and forty years later, The Francis Frith Collection continues in the same innovative tradition and is now one of the foremost publishers of vintage photographs in the world. Some of the current activities include:

INTERIOR DECORATION

Today Frith's photographs can be seen framed and as giant wall murals in thousands of pubs, restaurants, hotels, banks, retail stores and other public buildings throughout the country. In every case they enhance the unique local atmosphere of the places they depict and provide reminders of gentler days in an increasingly busy and frenetic world.

PRODUCT PROMOTIONS

Frith products are used by many major companies to promote the sales of their own products or to reinforce their own history and heritage. Frith promotions have been used by Hovis bread, Courage beers, Scots Porage Oats, Colman's mustard, Cadbury's foods, Mellow Birds coffee, Dunhill pipe tobacco, Guinness, and Bulmer's Cider.

GENEALOGY AND FAMILY HISTORY

As the interest in family history and roots grows world-wide, more and more people are turning to Frith's photographs of Great Britain for images of the towns, villages and streets where their ancestors lived; and, of course, photographs of the churches and chapels where their ancestors were christened, married and buried are an essential part of every genealogy tree and family album.

FRITH PRODUCTS

All Frith photographs are available Framed or just as Mounted Prints and unmounted versions. These may be ordered from the address below. Other products available are - Calendars, Jigsaws, Canvas Prints, Mugs, Tea Towels, Tableware and local and prestige books.

THE INTERNET

Over several hundred thousand Frith photographs can be viewed and purchased on the internet through the Frith websites!

For more detailed information on Frith products, look at
www.francisfrith.com

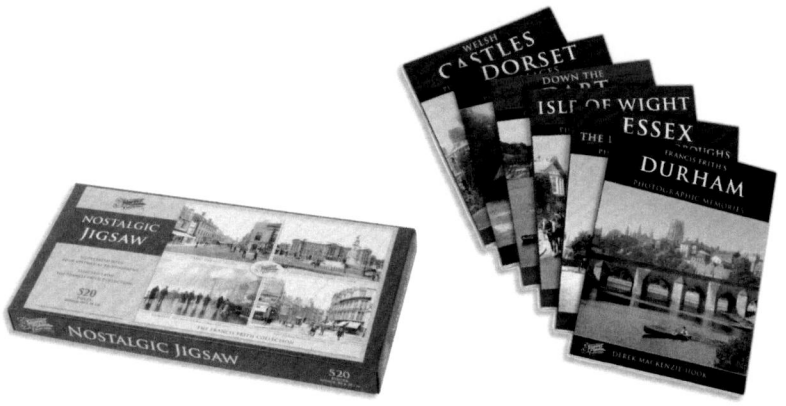
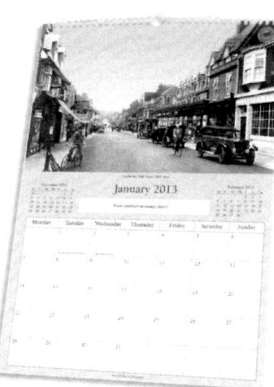

See the complete list of Frith Books at: www.francisfrith.com
This web site is regularly updated with the latest list of publications from The Francis Frith Collection. If you wish to buy books relating to another part of the country that your local bookshop does not stock, you may purchase on-line.

For further information, trade, or author enquiries please contact us at the address below:
The Francis Frith Collection, Unit 19 Kingsmead Business Park, Gillingham, Dorset SP8 5FB.
Tel: +44 (0)1722 716 376   Email: sales@francisfrith.co.uk

See Frith products on the internet at www.francisfrith.com

FREE PRINT OF YOUR CHOICE
CHOOSE A PHOTOGRAPH FROM THIS BOOK
+ POSTAGE

Mounted Print
Overall size 14 x 11 inches (355 x 280mm)

TO RECEIVE YOUR FREE PRINT

Choose any Frith photograph in this book
Simply complete the Voucher opposite and return it with your payment (to cover postage and handling) and we will print the photograph of your choice in SEPIA (size 11 x 8 inches) and supply it in a cream mount ready to frame (overall size 14 x 11 inches).

Order additional Mounted Prints at HALF PRICE - £19.00 each (normally £38.00)
If you would like to order more Frith prints from this book, possibly as gifts for friends and family, you can buy them at half price (with no additional postage costs).

Have your Mounted Prints framed
For an extra £20.00 per print you can have your mounted print(s) framed in an elegant polished wood and gilt moulding, overall size 16 x 13 inches (no additional postage required).

IMPORTANT!

❶ Please note: aerial photographs and photographs with a reference number starting with a "Z" are not Frith photographs and cannot be supplied under this offer.

❷ Offer valid for delivery to one UK address only.

❸ These special prices are only available if you use this form to order. You must use the ORIGINAL VOUCHER on this page (no copies permitted). We can only despatch to one UK address.

❹ This offer cannot be combined with any other offer.

As a customer your name & address will be stored by Frith but not sold or rented to third parties. Your data will be used for the purpose of this promotion only.

Send completed Voucher form to:
**The Francis Frith Collection,
1 Chilmark Estate House, Chilmark,
Salisbury, Wiltshire SP3 5DU**

Voucher for FREE and Reduced Price Frith Prints

Please do not photocopy this voucher. Only the original is valid, so please fill it in, cut it out and return it to us with your order.

Picture ref no	Page no	Qty	Mounted @ £19.00	Framed + £20.00	Total Cost £
		1	Free of charge*	£	£
			£19.00	£	£
			£19.00	£	£
			£19.00	£	£
			£19.00	£	£
			£19.00	£	£

Please allow 28 days for delivery. Offer available to one UK address only.

* Post & handling	£3.80
Total Order Cost	£

Title of this book ....

I enclose a cheque/postal order for £ ....
made payable to 'Heritage Resource Management Ltd'

OR please debit my Mastercard / Visa / Maestro card, details below

Card Number:

Issue No (Maestro only):   Valid from (Maestro):

Card Security Number: Expires:

Signature:

Name Mr/Mrs/Ms ....
Address ....
....
....
.... Postcode ....
Daytime Tel No ....
Email ....

Valid to 31/12/26

Free Print – see overleaf

Can you help us with information about any of the Frith photographs in this book?

We are gradually compiling an historical record for each of the photographs in the Frith archive. It is always fascinating to find out the names of the people shown in the pictures, as well as insights into the shops, buildings and other features depicted.

If you recognize anyone in the photographs in this book, or if you have information not already included in the author's caption, do let us know. We would love to hear from you, and will try to publish it in future books or articles.

An Invitation from The Francis Frith Collection to Share Your Memories

The 'Share Your Memories' feature of our website allows members of the public to add personal memories relating to the places featured in our photographs, or comment on others already added. Seeing a place from your past can rekindle forgotten or long held memories. Why not visit the website, find photographs of places you know well and add YOUR story for others to read and enjoy? We would love to hear from you!

www.francisfrith.com/memories

Our production team

Frith books are produced by a small dedicated team at offices near Salisbury. Most have worked with the Frith Collection for many years. All have in common one quality: they have a passion for the Frith Collection.

Frith Books and Gifts

We have a wide range of books and gifts available on our website utilising our photographic archive, many of which can be individually personalised.

www.francisfrith.com